AMISH
Ways

Amish Ways
Text © 1991 by Ruth Hoover Seitz
Photographs © 1991 by Blair Seitz
ISBN 1-879441-77-2

Library of Congress Catalog Card
Number 90-063838

SUMMARY: Eight text subjects and 150
photographs present Amish ways in
three Anabaptist settlements; Lancaster
County, Pennsylvania, eastern Ohio, &
Ontario, Canada. 120 pp.

Published by

BOOKS

Seitz and Seitz, Inc.
1006 N. Second St., Suite 1-A
Harrisburg, PA 17102-3121

Design by Master Designs, Palmyra, PA

Printed in Hong Kong
second printing

AMISH Ways

by Ruth Hoover Seitz
Photography by Blair Seitz

RB
BOOKS
HARRISBURG, PA

Acknowledgments

This book is rooted in a picture memory. Pigtailed, I was standing in long white stockings, black shoes and a homemade Sunday dress in front of my Grandma's grained corner cupboard. I was handing her delicate, pretty dishes that had been used to serve several sours and at least seven sweets at a family dinner. The table had been set three times to accommodate all the great aunts and second cousins. Grandma Hoover handled the dishes as carefully as she maintained connection with all her relatives. For her, posessing the keepsakes paled against recollecting the giver and the occasion. For my Mennonite grandmother, belonging was paramount.

Belonging is the foundation of Amish culture. It creates love. It gives Amish people the fortitude to give up individual preferences for community standards. In return for obedience, an Amish person receives cradle to grave security and the rewards of being a part.

For all the Amish who have shared their lives, concerns and delights, I am grateful for your time and openness. I thank you for the ways your faith strengthened mine. I offer you anonymity, varying names and details to preserve that.

To others who have lent your insights and experiences with the Amish, I appreciate your willingness to share out of extensive research and inner reflections. I thank Si and Esta Hershberger, Walnut Creek, Ohio; Penny Armstrong CNM, Lancaster, PA; Jay and Liz Augspurger, Kidron, Ohio; Urie Bender, Baden, Ontario; Orland Gingerich, Kitchener, Ontario; Maribel Kraybill, Lancaster, PA; Martha Hartzler Rohrer CNM, Harrisonburg, VA: and Joanne Siegrist, Bird in Hand, PA.

I thank several organizations who kindly assisted with some aspect of this project: The Amish Homestead, Lancaster, PA; Amish Farm and House, Lancaster, PA; The German Culture Museum, Walnut Creek, OH; The Mennonite Historical Society, The Mennonite Information Center, both in Lancaster, PA and the Pequea Bruderschaft Library, Intercourse, PA.

When I think of the process of shaping this text, I concur with the words of an Amish farmer, "Nothing is really work unless you'd rather be doing something else." And to our daughters, Charmaine and Renee, thanks for doing meals cheerfully when it must have seemed like work because you really wanted to be doing something else.

_____ Ruth Hoover Seitz

Born Into A Tradition

Sheets of rain pelted the blacktop of a country road in Lancaster County. Elam pulled his black wide-brimmed Amish hat down hard and ran as though his life depended on it. His wife's might. She had sounded earnest. You're getting a little beside yourself, he thought. With the first four children, Katie did just fine. His thoughts raced on. Nobody else was out at this hour of the night. The kitchen clock had struck two when Katie had tapped his arm and told him he'd better go. This rain was a surprise and just what his alfalfa needed. He was glad he didn't have to get somebody up to use a phone. A half mile down the road, he slipped into an Amish phone shed and dialed the number of the midwife. She answered. With relief he blurted, "Katie needs you—*now*."

"Is this Elam from near Ronks?" the midwife asked.

"Yes." It was harder to talk on the phone than in person. It felt strange. The phone had been in their neighborhood since 1988 when John B's wife had a heart attack. He and Katie share the use and expense with four other Old Order Amish families. A phone in this society is for essentials and stays outside the home so it won't intrude on family life. The Amish are a plain people noticeable for their unadorned style of dress; horse-drawn vehicles and implements; family-centered lifestyle and small-scale technology. Faith in God and belief in church traditions determine Amish ways.

The midwife wanted details about Katie's condition, but in his haste, Elam had forgotten to go over the list of signs with his wife. Despite his oversight, she agreed to come.

PREPARATION HOMESTYLE

Back in the house, Katie was up and busy. She had set out the kitchen scales and adjusted a pie board and blanket on top to weigh the baby at birth. Water was on to boil. She was washing and cutting rhubarb stalks that had been standing in the washhouse overnight. "I might even have time to put these into pies." she said. Noticing that Elam was looking at her a little puzzled as he washed up, she added, "Things have slowed down a little. But we'll need the crib this morning." Getting it down from the attic was usually one of the last-minute tasks. Amish parents tend to keep quiet about a new baby sister or brother coming and keep the crib out of sight.

"I sure hope it comes before milking time," said Elam. The cows would wait a little while, but six o'clock was the latest.

A solid no-nonsense woman, Katie paused to breathe as a contraction tore through her strong frame. Then she dipped flour out of a large tin and dropped a dollop of lard into the bowl. She set some cold water nearby. In popped Bonnie, the midwife. "I was just about to start pie dough, but let me get you some tea." Katie was one of those who bustled around until the crown of the head showed, so the midwife suggested she check her first and see how far she was dilated.

Katie agreed, Plastic and clean sheets were already on the bed. Homemade pads lay on the chest where they had been stored. A crib and Elam were thumping down the wooden stairs as quietly as possible.

"No time for pie-making," Bonnie insisted. "I'm going to scrub."

"I need a shower," Katie popped up from the bed, but slowed for a contraction. It passed and she talked on. "I'm glad I picked over the strawberries yesterday. There won't be ripe ones for a few days. My sister said she and her girls will help with the peas." Amish women consider birthing a baby a natural and ordinary experience. They stay oriented to the whole family, often keeping tabs on their housework. As the length of time between contractions shortened, Elam put a chair underneath the doorknob to prevent an early riser from bursting in on the action.

A GIFT FROM GOD

In any of the 175 Amish settlements across North America, it is not uncommon for a woman to have ten children—nor to have a preschooler and grandchildren. Children are a gift from God, worthy of loving acceptance but not fussy pride.

Amish families consider a deformed child a special gift from God. With gentleness, the parents of a newborn with EVC dwarfism, an untreatable congenital condition, accept their baby. Through intermarriage over more than 200 years, everyone in the community

5

is liable to be a carrier of the gene. There are as many EVC dwarfs among Lancaster Amish as exist in the rest of the world. As adults, deformed people find valuable income-generating work in the Amish community.

An hour later, light slowly crawled from the eastern horizon. Sweaty exhaustion lined Katie's face and dampened her nightie. Elam held her hand, talking very low in Dutch. Bonnie remembered that he had sat on four inches of the bed, ready to bolt, when their firstborn was on her way seven years ago. He was an excellent labor assistant, doing exactly what Bonnie told him without challenging her reasoning or voicing inadequacy. Amish men will give their utmost to prevent their wives from delivering in the hospital. That expensive realm with puzzling technology overwhelms them; however, they do arrange for hospitalization when needed. Fear of the complexities of a hospital delivery has prompted some young husbands in Lancaster to attend childbirth classes.

Little feet pattered down the stairway, and the knob jiggled. *Bleib draus,* whispered Elam, telling the child in Pennsylvania Dutch, the Amish dialect, to stay out.

When Bonnie urged Katie to push, she guided the head and shoulders of a pink-skinned infant out of the birth canal. Katie sighed and squeezed Elam's hand. Their look showed gratitude that it was over and all was well. He spoke a few words to the baby but left shortly because the cows were bawling, insisting on their own relief.

Within a half hour, Katie rocked a clean, healthy little boy, gently touching his miniature fingertips and introducing him to Dutch. After she had cleaned up, Bonnie put the baby to the breast.

A FAMILY WELCOME

The children came downstairs, all dressed with each other's help. They gathered round, the little ones touching their mother with shy wonder, trying to make sure that she was still the same. Katie spoke to each one, understanding their need. Then she affirmed, "We're all hungry, just like the baby. Marian, get out the cereal and milk. There is a bowl of strawberries in the refrigerator. All was set out on the cloth covering on the wide table in the middle of the kitchen. While the newborn was on her second breast, Katie's sister and girls arrived with a baby nurse, someone who would handle the housework for a few days. A neighbor stopped in as well as Katie's aunt. After the birth, everybody was welcome with no particular visiting hours.

They named him Benjamin, after Elam's uncle. For a short while, he wore dresses. He soaked in attention and touch while he lay in an infant seat on the big table where so much happened. There his extended family visited; his siblings played games under the hanging pressure lantern; his mother rolled out cookies; snapped beans and cut material to make her family's clothes. He sat on somebody's lap during church; and was carried outside with the older ones while his mother worked in the garden. His toys were simple, so he could be creative. By the time he had a little sister, Benjamin clearly loved books. Sometimes he'd ask his mother, "Doesn't Mary need to drink?' Mom would read him books while she nursed child number six, just as important as the rest.

Amish children work hard compared to non-Amish, but they learn their work gradually in a manner that builds their self-esteem and sense of belonging.

PASSING IT ON

I observed such parenting when I dropped by to help Katie an afternoon six weeks before Benjamin was born. Katie had decided that we would wash the toys. For her three oldest, this was a grand adventure--for the seven-year-old because it was a variation from washing dishes and for the younger two, it seemed almost like doing dishes, a responsibility they anticipate. They put on their aprons and set their stools at the sink and washed, rinsed and dried all the plastic and wooden toys emptied from the toy chest and shelves. When they grew weary, their mother accepted their wish to play outdoors. They left the scene with no dislike for the task. Washing dishes was something they like to do because their mother does it. Amish parents believe it is normal for their children to follow what they do. They carefully mind their own actions so that their children will have an exemplary model.

In their desire for their children to absorb Amish ways, parents keep their young ones in isolation so they are spared exposure to worldliness. I overheard a mother commenting that she didn't want her preschoolers to look at the pictures in a certain library book. She did not want them to integrate information conflicting with their beliefs into their young minds. Lifestyle standards and family experiences often work together to support Amish offspring growing up in a faith tradition

On a late summer day I stopped by her add-on apartment to hear stories about mementoes that Fannie King had kept over her 77 years. She was bent over her lap quilting, the afternoon window light deepening the dark blue of her cape dress. The sun angled across the linoleum, striking the corner cupboard that Fannie's grandmother Leah had received from her parents when she married in 1855.

A corner cupboard of fancy dishes commemorates family experiences. From its corner in many Amish kitchens in Lancaster, this piece of furniture is a safe for "pretty things" that are keepsakes.

Fannie explained that several large pieces of Depression glass were in the bags of flour that her mother had bought when she peddled baked goods door to door in the city 70 years ago.

Fannie carefully lifted a bone animal that looked like a deer. "My father called it a *gasbuck*, which means mountain goat. At the end of our meal in honor of my parents' fiftieth anniversary, my father asked for the wishbones from the birds that his daughter-in-law had roasted. He made the antlers from the goose's wishbone and used the two chicken wishbones for the legs, gluing soybeans for eyes."

"Oh, this is something that my mother made for each of her 25 grandchildren." On her mid-finger Ann dangled a loop attached to a yarn-covered cube that rattled. "No one ever guessed that the noise came from BBs in a duck's windpipe. She got the idea from her own mother who had made this rattle for me." She held up a colorful ball with very fine crocheting.

For the Amish, there is a continuity of values and skills from generation to generation just as family keepsakes are passed on.

Keeping Their Faith as a Community

"It's such a beautiful day," Anna murmured softly as we headed towards an Amish church service on a glowing Indian summer morning. In the well-mulched flower beds we passed along this uneven two-lane Ohio road, firebranch, impatiens and geraniums still bloomed tall as if to defy any threat of frost. We waved to families in the solid colors of Amish garb walking leisurely along the roadside. My friends, Anna and Abe, knew which church district each group belonged to and surmised which house they were going to for worship. We were driving to a New Order Amish church service. This group separated from the Old Order to conduct more youth activities, frowning on smoking and drinking that is tolerated by many Old Order districts.

Workhorses grazed during their weekly break from fieldwork, and a few yearlings rolled in the sun. Lush meadows and corn rows with plump ears extended from neat farmsteads with silos and sizable houses. Even non-farming Amish build homes large enough to seat over a hundred people because each family takes a turn at having church.

CHURCH IN HOMES—A RADICAL TRADITION

We drew up in front of a neat brick suburban house. How could the hosts, Aaron and Lizzie Ann Hershberger, accommodate the horses and buggies of the thirty families who comprise this church district? Horses pastured and neighed behind the small barn, and men parked their clean, snappy black buggies in the adjoining yard of a married son.

At church the Amish tend to socialize with their own age groups. Abe disappeared into a group of gray-bearded men while Anna and I stepped into the basement to join the older Amish women. Each wore a long-sleeved solid-colored dress with a white organdy apron over the long skirt and a prayer covering doing just that to their long hair wound into a bun. Without makeup, their skin glowed with healthy freshness. Each person's dress defined their belonging to the Amish just as their horse and carriage transportation overruled individual stature by equalizing status. Besides dress and horse-drawn transportation, their speaking to each other in Pennsylvania Dutch unites the Amish under a community umbrella that separates them from the world.

After putting down her bonnet identified with magic marker inside as, "Abe's Anna", she greeted Lizzie Ann with a handshake and a holy kiss,"a token of love for your brothers and sisters in faith," she explained. Soon after a clock chimed nine, females came down from the main floor, their black stockings and shoes appearing first. Following the married women came the singles with black prayer coverings, and finally girls in white pinafores. Mothers with little ones sat farthest from the speaker who would stand in a space without flowers or podium between two groups of facing benches. Speaking from an unmarked area seems to accentuate the role of Amish leaders as servants.

A few rocking chairs upstairs still squeaked as infants breastfed. Like a developing mime, men shuffled in from the yard, first the white bearded ones filling the long benches facing the women. The overflow sat on shorter wooden benches, all constructed by the members. Combing their hair, teen boys in white shirts and layered hairstyles crossed the threshold looking more mainstream than any of the other age groups. The men removed their hats. Several people passed out small German hymnbooks, the *Lieder sammiung*, that were stored in a wooden box. A sense of gatheredness settled in.

SINGING IN GERMAN

Out of the quiet, a male voice began singing in German in a high quavering chant, and after one prolonged phrase, the congregation joined in. The group held onto each sound, the slow flow of the words reminding me of the seventeenth century madrigals I sang with a group in school. I closed my eyes and imagined their persecuted forebearers singing these same words from the *Ausbund,* a German hymnbook, in a more secretive underground setting in Europe three hundred years ago. Since then, these tunes have travelled by word of mouth down through the generations. During a twenty-minute song, I relaxed deeply, the words soothing like a mantra.

During the first song, the bishop, a deacon and a minister went out for "council" or to discuss the order of the service and any discipline matters. Anna told me that when each of her children wanted to become a church member, they followed the leaders out of the service and began a period of instruction leading to baptism.

The first sermon came forth in German with the English repeated for my benefit. The minister's text, given without notes, began at the core of Amish theology—submitting to God and the guidance of the Church to deny the flesh and the world. Expounding on Titus 1 in the New Testament, the gray-bearded man described the pride of life; the lust of the eye and the lust of the flesh as aspects of the world. He spoke kindly but pointedly, "There's nothing hid that God will not find." He closed on a positive note, "God fulfills His promises; our duty is to be faithful." Being faithful meant following the Bible and the *Ordnung*, largely unwritten guidelines to living Amish.

PRACTICING LOVE

A caring spirit and a sense of direction from the *Ordnung* and its Biblical backdrop bound this group together. I felt it while kneeling on the throw carpets for silent prayer. Whenever the one-year-old with a Gerber baby face threw her stiff covering to the floor with childish abandon, her mother waited before putting it on her head, preventing the child's action from becoming a game or an independent gesture. By slipping it back on gently, the mother showed her young one the Amish way.

A young mother handed their toddler to her husband. The father took her eagerly while a look of mutual support passed between this parental team. My mind returned to the ardent voice of the white-bearded bishop. He directed his attention to the men, seeming to avoid glancing toward the left, the women's section. His Pennsylvania Dutch rang through the basement, almost joyfully. When his voice switched to the cadence of German poetry, his bowl-shaped head of hair bobbing slowly, I felt like I was in the presence of a prayerful monk. The bishop's memory also served him when he realized he had no glasses and could not read his Bible.

After two and a half hours of sitting, the little children fussed and refused playthings, even pretzels,

and the pregnant women looked flushed even though they had accepted seats near an open window. Another kneeling prayer ending with the bishop's audible, "Amen" and a standing benediction finished the church service. The youngest up to the oldest, first the females and then the males, filed upstairs and outdoors.

LUNCH FOLLOWS WORSHIP

The church district's property included a wooden box of inexpensive table ware; the trunk of songbooks, and the benches. Stored in a specially-sized wagon, these necessities rotated among the homes holding church. In contrast to maintaining a half-million dollar building, the Amish way illustrates that they view life as a journey to a heavenly land with godliness within the community more important than a structure.

After a communal meal, similar to the one I would experience later in Lancaster, the group evaporated slowly. We shook hands goodbye, a silent activity. Effusiveness, even delight, were not a part of this group experience. There were no shouts of glee from two little boys in white shirts and dark trousers swinging on the hitching rail outside the horse barn. The Lord's Day is for worship, rest, and visiting. Anna confirmed this by saying she felt like taking a nap. "Maybe you'd like to do the same," she offered. As I lay down in her spare room, most frequently used by visiting grandchildren, I slipped away to the patter of hoofs and the scrape of buggy wheels on dirt roads as families drove home from church at a house.

Practices that identify the Amish as a people draw them together and accentuate their differences from mainstream culture. Accepted ways—for example, men growing beards after marriage; youth finishing formal schooling at age fourteen; houses without television, radios and stereos and farmers using draft power to pull implements through the fields—all build parameters that help the Amish to live humbly, gently and peacefully with God's people and earth.

9

Finding A Place to Practice Their Faith

The scent of brewed coffee rose with the German benediction at the end of another Amish church service in Lancaster. Among these plain folks, families, not individuals, are counted as members. And like the Ohio service all stayed for the cold meal served after church. This bi-weekly tradition reflects love, simplicity and orderliness.

A SIMPLE REPAST

The young people stood around a table in the kitchen. In the basement, men made up tables by placing two benches atop handcrafted leg props Benches also served as seats. In Amishland women are in charge of food.

The menu and the manner of serving were routine. Out of wooden boxes came coffeecups, plastic tumblers for water and knives. Ham and cheese, sliced homemade bread, mayonnaise, pickled cucumbers and redbeets and peanut butter mixed with Karo syrup—four plates of each—stretched the length of each of two tables, one for the ordained and older men and the other for married women. These sandwich fixings were within the reach of each person. Some older people declined to serve themselves a beet with a knife. Only a coffee pot and milk were passed along the rows. Pies made with *snitz* or dried apples topped off the lunch.

My own familiarity with Pennsylvania Dutch fare prompted me to tuck slices of bread and butter pickles into my ham and cheese sandwich. The fluffy bread was tastier than store brands.

No vegetables or fruits appeared. Six-year-old Mabel beside me didn't seem to mind. She quietly nibbled the quarter sandwiches that her *mommy* , the Pennsylvania Dutch word for grandmother, folded from half slices of bread. People visited with relaxed humility, sharing news from relatives in other settlements; offering surplus spinach and talking about the next parents' meeting for an Amish one-room school. A sense of yielding, of deferring to God and others pervaded interactions. I didn't notice anyone going for self-promotion or distinction from the rest. Service rather than one upmanship characterizes the Amish way.

For centuries their homes have been the center for worship as well as teaching and practicing obedience, faith and service. Children gain understanding of Amish ways from the time they are born in their parents' bedroom to the closing of life when families clothe the deceased in white burial garb before a home funeral. Families use their homes to visit, work, worship and sing. Within the walls young people socialize and get married, and relatives celebrate and share work projects.

THEIR REFORMATION ROOTS

From the sixteenth century, a radical religious group in Europe called Anabaptists, had been punished, even killed, for illegally gathering in their homes to study the Bible rather than attend the state church. These courageous Christians based church membership—and re-baptism—on a faith in Christ that influenced all of their actions. They rejected infant baptism, a practice sanctioned by early reformers of the Catholic Church, Ulrich Zwingli and Martin Luther. Anabaptists refused to fight or resist power and upheld church and state being separate entities.

The efforts of the Anabaptists to form a fellowship directed by the Bible in all aspects of their lives drew them to refuse communion to any member who broke the baptismal vow and to excommunicate those who continued to do wrong. II Thessalonians 3:14 is one of several Bible verses prompting *Bann* and *Meidung* , translated in English as excommunication and shunning. "...if any man obey not our word by this epistle, note that man, and have no company with him, that he may be ashamed." This mode of discipline was taught by Menno Simons, a leader whose followers in the Netherlands were called Mennonites.

In 1694, Jakob Ammann, another Anabaptist leader in Bern, Switzerland, advocated a stricter *Meidung*. He insisted that fallen members be forbidden to eat, travel or do business with faithful members and founded a group of followers who became known as Amish.

Differences in dress and lifestyle came to characterize this Anabaptist subgroup. And ever since the Amish emigrated to the New World in the early 1700s, disagreements about specifcs have led to migrations, splits and new groups of plain people. Each branch draws a chalkline to designate how far from the modern world their practices must lie.

In Ohio, for example, the Swartzentruber Amish support inconvenience as a form of simplicity. They forego running water and drive carriages without windows. They do not hire Amish taxis, vehicles that transport Amish to distant relatives, etc., but spend long hours together at church and lose few of their members to more liberal groups. In contrast, the New Order Amish hold Sunday School and some venture abroad and stay in hotels to learn more about Biblical and Anabaptist history. The New Order also plan supervised activities rather than granting their youth license for an experimental fling before joining church, as the Old Order groups do. Those who leave the New Order often adopt a church group that uses electricity and tractor power.

PUSHING WESTWARD TO OHIO

In 1810 Amish pioneers forged their wagons over the worn footpath to settle in eastern Ohio. Millers, now the most common Amish surname in Ohio, as well as Stutzmans, Yoders and Troyers pushed west from Somerset County in southwestern Pennsylvania beyond the Ohio River to settle wilderness available in 160-acre portions for $2.00 an acre.

Thorough land scouting as early as 1807 led these Amish farmers to select bottomlands along the Sugar and Walnut Creeks. These major creeks offered waterpower and, feeder streams threaded through loamy lands. The settlers prized the hillsides of sturdy hardwoods, especially the black walnut trees that they preferred for cabins. As they plunged into the task of building shelter and growing food for themselves and their animals, they must have worked with gratitude for a safe place to farm and worship. (("History of the Amish Settlement" by Leroy Beachy, presented at Symposium "Amish in Eastern Ohio", The German Culture Museum, Walnut Creek, Ohio, June 22-23, 1990. Used by permission.)

Six generations earlier, their ancestors had moved several times in Europe to escape harsh governments and neighbors. Leaving the Alsace and Palatinate in the early eighteenth century, Mennonites and Amish ventured across the Atlantic to plant new roots in William Penn's "Peaceable Kingdom." It is not certain when the first Amish arrived. But immigrants arriving in 1737 contributed to the first two Amish settlements in the New World. Most moved to the valley at the base of the Blue Mountains in Berks County. Due to Indian raiding and crop failure, this colony fell apart but fed the three Somerset County settlements who later pushed into Ohio.

Some Amish remained in Pennsylvania's lush Lancaster County, now the home of more than sixteen thousand Old Order adults and children(*The Riddle of Amish Culture.* by Donald B. Kraybill Baltimore: The John Hopkins University Press, 1989 Used by permission). Today more than half of Pennsylvania's Amish live in Lancaster's countryside. This Eden, America's most productive, non-irrigated land, fed by limestone creeks and superb farm practices is now home to 94 Old Order districts. When a district becomes too large for a home, a new one based on road boundaries forms.

CANADA'S PROMISED LAND FOR THE AMISH

By 1822 Lancaster's farmland was too costly for Christian Nafziger, a peasant Amish farmer from Bavaria who had wound his way to the Commonwealth via New Orleans. With support from his brethren in faith, he headed northward to seek cheaper land in Canada. This determined man left what is now Toronto with a promise from the governor that any German settler who came and built a cabin would be granted 50 acres free with the opportunity to buy the rest of the plot at $2.50 an acre. News of this promised land circulated, and by 1824 Amish-Mennonites from Europe arrived at this thick wilderness, 40,000 acres known as The German Block. A few trickled in from Pennsylvania.

These first Germans to come to Canada settled in Wilmot Township directly west of Kitchener-Waterloo. They bore names such as Lichty, Kropf, Schultz, Litwiller, Gingerich and Brenneman. They enjoyed warm relations with the Government and neighbors of other religious groups. After half a century of peacefulness among themselves, disagreements led to a series of divisions, a major one on building meetinghouses rather than worshipping in homes.

In the 1950s before the US Supreme Court granted the Amish parochial school rights, groups from various states migrated to Canada for the freedom to have their own neighborhood schools, and settled close to the US border.

Farming With A Family Focus

After winding around Holmes County's sharp bends, I came upon a white barn hugging a steep hill in rural Ohio. The Yoder farmstead stood in golden relief in the late afternoon sun. I parked beside two buggies and peered into the milkhouse to look for Amos, head of household. Above the roaring generator that runs the milkers, his son Noah pointed toward the hill. "He's picking up ears of corn in one of those fields." After cutting corn stalks for making silage, someone returns to the field to pick up ears dropped from the wagon.

I headed up a steep field, driving across corn stubble. There was no stooping figure in sight as my car crested two hills. Back at the house, Amos was just finishing his 4:30 supper. Perhaps Noah hadn't wanted me to find his father. After all, I might draw him away from helping with the milking. Sixty-year-old Amos was decreasing his dairy involvement. His sons were the reason. "Noah has a way of making cows produce milk, and Benjamin handles their breeding. We're increasing the third of our herd that is registered. The fifth one works with a siding installation crew, but he owns a few cows and trains standardbred race horses to pull a buggy. And the oldest one would rather have greasy hands than farm. Each one should pursue what he's interested in."

THE WAIT FOR A FARM

Amos himself had waited many years to farm. Farms are now scarce in eastern Ohio, especially for the Amish who average seven children per family. Working for a carpenter and then a mason while his young family grew, he always kept his ears perked for an available farm. "It wasn't until 1974 when Elias, the oldest of our six boys, was thirteen that we bought this place from an 'English' farmer." Amos talked low, his eyes penetrating and his words humble as we sat down at the kitchen table, already cleared with the supper dishes in the cupboard. Self-consciousness flushed his cheeks down to his thin beard. "I heard about this place on Friday, looked at it on Saturday and bought it Monday." He said it with steadiness, and I knew this man had felt led with no rashness in his decision-making.

Eleven-year-old Edward looked up from his lessons, eager to hear about things that happened before he was born. He cares for the farm's smaller animals—feeding calves, rabbits and cats. "Wouldn't you like to have a kitten?" he had asked soon after I sat on a bench behind the table.

ARE SONS VITAL FOR AMISH FARMING?

Amos answered only what I asked. "No, we wouldn't have done it if we had had all girls. A farm teaches our Amish boys to work hard and to manage well." He smiled at his wife Ellen who was ironing shirts vigorously with a gas-fueled iron. A circle of blue flame heated the smooth back of the iron.

I thought of the Ervin Mast family with four girls and another baby due the end of this month. Renting a farm less than a year, they plan to do some hard thinking if the new one is a girl. Ervin said, "They can help with the milking and some fieldwork. There *are* advantages for the girls themselves. Girls who grow up on a farm don't shy away from harnessing a horse; they are assertive about handling the unexpected."

When they first bought the farm, the Yoders set themselves and their boys on a rigorous learning course. Amos drew on his boyhood experiences and got information from successful farmer friends.

"The first year was a nightmare," Ellen said. "We lost two horses to azoturia, and missed out on the timing of some fieldwork." Amos remembers that when he couldn't make a loan payment, his friend tore up the note and erased the debt. His eyes teared when he mentioned this kindness.

Then his voice lightened, "After the second year, we felt the blessings that we had been receiving all the time." One is the practice of mutual aid that Amish families share. Besides helping those who have accidents and losses, they incorporate work-sharing into their farm life. To work for mutual benefit with people you know is a pleasure—one that tops being together on the golf course, in Amish opinion.

THE SILO-FILLING RING

Uniting muscle power in Amishland is not only a social benefit; it is essential because the *Ordnung* forbids using self-propelled implements such as tractors and haybines. Amish do use a stationary steel-wheeled tractor as a power unit for filling silos, threshing wheat and running hydraulic systems, but animal power pulls whatever moves across the fields and down the roads. Using field tractors may easily lead to driving them on the road to pick up something. Driving cars would come next.

The Amish want to operate in a way that keeps things simple, slower and apart from the the world. They hold onto labor-intensive farming so that their families can work together. One farmer who rented tractor power to bring in his alfalfa in a pinch told me how difficult it was going to be to go back to horse-power this year. "If I don't, the ministers will be visiting us." The church community provides the social and physical support to follow the Amish way.

The silo-filling ring that replenished Yoders' 55-foot silo with chopped corn yesterday shortened an exhausting job. Eleven pairs of hands worked all day starting at 7:30 in the morning. The previous day Amos had cut his corn with the binder and corded the ear-laden stalks into sheaves. The corn was prime for silage—large ears with the kernels dented, and the stalks fairly green but wilting. As a team of horses pulled a wagon across the fields, three men tossed sheaves aboard while three others stacked the stalks several feet high. Two other loaded wagons were at the back of the barn where five other men pushed it into the chopper that also blew it up into the silo. The ensilage cutter was manufactured in the fifties. The men in the ring handle it with tender loving care, occasionally going to one of several Amish businesses that piece together and repair outdated implements. Moving from one farm to another, the men work until everybody's silo is filled. At each farm, the wife and daughters prepare to fill the stomachs of this hard-working crew.

When the silo is full, the remainder of the corn crop dries in the field a month longer. Workhorses, at least four, pull a machine that picks the ears, rides them up a short elevator to drop onto a wagon trailing behind. A diesel engine powers the machine. An airy crib stores the ears. A baler chops the stalks for fodder for the winter.

In Lancaster, a few farmers still raise wheat, selling the grain to a local mill and bedding their horses with the straw. "Wheat is grueling," commented Gideon Beiler, a seasoned farmer.

A wheat threshing ring—ideally, at least eight people— starts after the morning milking and works steadily except for dinner and an afternoon treat. After the grain is weighed and sold, the farmer with the highest yield per acre "gets bounced on for a treat."

Everybody who helped is invited to that home for an evening of sweet and salty snacks and visiting, a pastime Amish always enjoy.

FARMLAND SQUEEZE

I like to park along a Lancaster road with no telephone or electricity wires, a signal that all properties are Amish. I soak in the quiet view and allow its serenity to restrain my fax-style schedule. Such roads are decreasing because factories sprout to take advantage of employees with a strong work ethic, and the Amish themselves install phones to serve their cottage industries. The fast-growing Amish population opts for home businesses as their farmland shrinks into high-priced industrial plots and luxury real estate. Isaiah, one bearded Amish grandfather said, "It was okay when the tourists came and left. But now that they have decided to move here; they're buying the land that our sons need to farm. Who can afford land at $5,000-$7,000 per acre for five sons?" The Amish lack breathing space to tend the earth and teach their families the same.

The land squeeze pressures individual farm families. I can see David Lapp seeding alfalfa with his two Belgian horses. Today he's helping his oldest son who has taken over the home farm, the 66 acres that his grandfather and *his* father ploughed and tilled. His two other sons moved out of this tourist belt near Intercourse to a more rural setting in the southern part of the County. Lydia and Susie, two married daughters, migrated north to Perry County, a recent Amish settlement. Lydia's husband constructs storage barns at home while Susie and Allan are nurturing a rundown farm they bought. The Amish tell me it takes five years to build up land depleted by commercial fertilizers and poor cropping practices. David told me recently that he's worried about his youngest son, Abner. He just married and still is employed by an "English," a term to designate non-Amish, machinist. "He is not interested in any woodcraft or even in having his own home business. He is comfortable working where he does, but he would really like to farm. And that would be the best place when he and his wife have children."

In Canada, the Amish have been able to acquire farms from non-Amish abandoning this livelihood. Unavailability of land forces Amish into business in order to live. This lifestyle is an invitation to prosperity and has strong repercussions for future generations.

Preparing Food from God's Earth

Autumn dried and shriveled the crisp greens of summer. Sun on the decaying browns in gardens and byways offered unusual warmth last Thursday. Before the harvest season closed, I drove to Sally's farmhouse to make chow chow with Amish and "English" friends. To chop and pickle a variety of vegetables seemed an appropriate way to mark the end of the growing season. For generations Amish women have preserved this mixture as a condiment for meat and potatoes meals. Each woman includes vegetables according to her own liking, usually following the recipe that she enjoyed during her growing years. The history of chow chow dips back into Chinese, English and German cuisines.

As I turned into the gravel driveway, Shep, the Eshes' collie barked with Emma and Mark appearing simultaneously through the back screendoor. I was surprised to see Emma, a first grader who hides her reading ability so she can feel equal with her classmates who are learning the abc's. She was home from school because of a tummyache; I assured her that the day's activities would make her feel better.

In the kitchen the busyness and warm feelings of a sisters' day were already circulating. Two large pots of carrots and onions steamed on the dark gas stove that is standard in an Amish kitchen. Several people joshed and chopped around a large improvised cutting board on the table in the center of the room. After hugs and handshakes, I set my jars in a corner; unwrapped my knives and joined the team. Esther, a young Amish mother with a sharp wit, handed me a brush to scrub cauliflower at the sink . She snapped off the florets and later the leaves from celery. The stalks of vegetables that we pulled from huge plastic bags had just been parted from their roots that morning. Esther and her husband raise produce for market auction.

THE MEDLEY OF SISTERS AND VEGETABLES

We all shared the work under Sally's supervision because our range of experience with chow chow varied widely. I, for one, had only chopped and tasted and wondered about the end of the process. After the cooked vegetables cooled, Sally dumped them into her special chow chow tub, large enough to hold dozens of gallons. Next we added rinsed, canned vegetables—

chick peas; green, Northern and kidney beans as well as tiny pickles that Sally had jarred during cucumber season. Everyone peered into the colorful mixture, getting more so as young Emma stirred the ten ingredients. "It's beautiful," we murmured, in awe of the cardinal red peppers against the large white beans. Someone missed corn kernels, but Sally explained, "I leave them out because corn makes it look milky."

Sally gasped, "Oh, I almost forgot the vinegar solution. Does anybody know how to make it?" Then it was our turn to be surprised. "Don't you have a recipe?" someone wondered.

"No, I just mix it until it tastes right." What humble confidence! None of us "English" had a clue about the amounts, and the Amish women seemed to accept Sally's way. It was a sure one. Indeed, throughout the winter I would remember Sally's method every time I enjoyed the superb sweet and sour of her chow chow.

We moved into the next shift of work. Someone opened the sugar bags and measured vinegar. Others washed and lined up their glass canning jars. Emma, Mark and I took a wagon to get wood for a fire under the big iron kettle where the jars would seal under a fifteen-minute boiling bath. Wood scraps from their father's carpentry shop filled a row of feed bags. We hauled one into the cement laundry room where Sally heats her wash water each week. On the porch, numerous farm kittens brushed by our feet, hoping to get some food before milking time. "Wouldn't you like one or two?" Sally begged. High birth rates in two areas seem to impact this cultural group!

FROM COLD PACKING TO THE BOILING BATH

Soon the first batch of jars were simmering in a boiling bath. Sally's eyes lit up. She had wiped the sticky table where the rest had packed each jar with a mixture of vegetables and baptized them with the pickling juice. "How about a game?" Outside on their way from the barn, five-year-old Rhoda was hanging onto her daddy's arm as she rollerskated on one foot. Ezra opened the door to Sally's tease, "Don't *you* know when to come to the house? We're just ready to start Pictionary ™."

Ezra stuck a toothpick between his lips, just above an untrimmed graying beard. The twinkle in his eyes revealed how much he liked to play. "Oh, you go ahead. I really should go back to the shop." But with some group coaxing, he stayed a little longer, making pointers from the sidelines. What lively evenings the Esches and their friends must have guessing drawings frantically sketched on discarded computer paper! It wasn't the first time I noticed what a highly developed sense of play flows within Amish families. Mark, the clockwatcher, interrupted the game. It was time to lift the first batch of chow chow from the canning kettle.

In the clear liquid, the vegetables gleamed brightly. After several more batches, each woman packed up her filled jars—despite the Plain Folks' mandate that they shouldn't be moved for 24 hours. We decided to forego that detail of the tradition because the whole day of working together like Amish sisters was the true value of making chow chow.

Helping each other can, freeze and pickle foods for the winter firms one's sense of belonging to a people, of being needed and worthy of receiving. The tasks of picking vegetables and fruits; snapping, shelling and creaming them and then boiling them in jars or packaging them for the freezer and doing all that when each is mature and ripe sounds overwhelming. Amish women manage this as successfully as an MBA implements a marketing plan for a manufacturer. And they do it with grace and confidence—and an acceptance of life as it unfolds.

LEARNING MOM'S WAYS

Their success relies on gradual hands-on training from childhood. A four-year-old is given some peas to put in her apron just as Mom does. She watches her older sisters open the pod and hustle the peas out with their thumb. She tries twisting the plump pod in half, but then it's hard to split the seam open. She works at a few, and her mother praises her efforts. "*Du konst voll!*" Her mother does not rebuke the little one when she dumps the rest of her peas in her sister's lap and goes outside to play wagon.

By the time a girl leaves eighth grade she is likely to have a grasp of the steps of freezing peas from knowing when and how to pick to taking the bags to the locker in town. (The Amish in Lancaster rent freezer space, but some in Holmes County use natural gas from wells on their properties to run freezers. Canadian Amish forego freezers.) When a girl leaves to set up housekeeping, she has handled the procedures on her own, but appreciates preserving with other family members.

Young Amish mothers who do income-generating work at home reduce the number of foods preserved and buy time-saving hand-operated devices to do the same job that their grandmothers did. Erma Stoltzfus sells quilts and decorator pillows from her house. She cans some food as an easy ingredient for a dish she makes regularly. She cans peas to put into chicken pies and seasoned tomato puree for pizza and spaghetti sauce. Other garden musts are sweet corn to be frozen creamed; tomatoes; onions; asparagus; strawberries; redbeets; applesauce and green beans.

To feed her growing family of five, she takes some shortcuts. She raises fresh carrots for her family with the horses getting their share. With tourists interrupting her work day, she doesn't can carrots like she used to. Unlike her mother, he hasn't made sauerkraut or relishes the last few years. She bakes bread only occasionally.

One day the sun dazzled across the shiny high apparatus steaming on Sarah Beiler's dark brown stove. It was the day for making and canning grape juice. Traditionally, this was a slow and messy process. Bees hovered around the cheesecloth bag that strained juice from cooked grapes all day on the washline. Then the juice had to be boiled for canning. But with the assistance of a new, pricey contraption imported from Scandinavia, this process would not take a whole day, only hours.

After fifteen-year-old Mary pulled off the rotten and green grapes, her mother washed the healthy bunches and packed them into the top of the steamer. As the water in the bottom boiled, its steam cooked the fruit of the vine. The essence of each grape dripped into the water, making a natural, flavorful juice.

After the pot boiled for an hour, it was time to pour the hot juice into jars to preserve for winter use. Just then the loud bell of the phone in the garage rang. In Amish suburbia, the flow of life has a few more interruptions than on the Amish farm. The phone was installed for emergencies and for Isaac to order materials for his woodworking shop. A home phone is taboo in many Old Order communities. With such a convenience, phone conversations would replace face-to-face visiting and would soil the rhythms of family togetherness.

Today Rachel, the second youngest, ran to answer. It was an English neighbor saying she was bringing a bushel of apples from her tree. "She could have just brought them," Sarah said in Dutch.

Just as she started to lower the hose attached to the steamer, five-month old Martha on the floor cried with frustration. All her toys were beyond her reach. The top of her homemade dress, all a plain fabric, was wet with teething dribble. Sarah lowered the gas flame and scooped up Martha, "You're ready for your nap." With acceptance of her little one's needs, this busy mother dropped into a rocking chair. Martha switched to a more contented tone as she started to nurse.

Lest the juice boil away, Sarah instructed her daughter to set a dishpan of clean two-quart jars on the stepstool and to open the clamp slowly to fill a jar at a time. "Won't the jars crack?" Mary wondered.

"Let the juice out slowly against the top side of the jar."

The teenager took hold of this new procedure, filling the jars; wiping the rims and then closing them with hot lids and bands that were simmering on the back burner. She was emptying the skins and stems onto the compost heap at the end of the garden when her mother returned to the kitchen from tucking Martha into her crib.

A mother and daughter is a team in expediting growing things from the farm to the table. In Amish culture, it is a female realm. Men who come to the kitchen at dinner but before the food is ready, sit and relax or play with the children. Each spouse accepts responsibility for his or her domain.

Learning Essentials; Omitting the Frills

Their straw hats and wide-brimmed bonnets sheltered their hair from the falling mist as Amish boys and girls strode along a dirt road to their parochial school near Millersburg, Ohio.

After many years of insisting that their children required a basic education in a neighborhood school and not the expanded and competitive curriculum of consolidated schools, Amish were granted by a 1972 Supreme Court order the right to hire teachers to teach the 3Rs in their own schools. It is not unusual to see one-room schoolhouses of yesteryear, complete with outhouses, woodstoves and pressure lanterns, dotting Amish settlements across North America. To visit is to step back about five decades to a learning setting that focuses on gaining the skills to read, write and do basic math.

By the time the warning bell rang at nine o'clock, most were in the basement hanging up their sweaters and placing their lunchboxes below on a bench. A two-seated carriage pulled up at the last minute. The sliding doors were pushed into their pockets, and children popped out from both sides and scrambled indoors. Mary Kline, a first year teacher of Grades 5-8, pulled a rope to ring the small shiny bell hanging from the door moulding. As promptly as its sound faded, all 25 scholars were seated in the same style wooden desks I sat in back in Pennsylvania during the early fifties.

"Good morning, students," smiled Mary.

"Good morning, teacher," they chorused softly. Without looking at a list, the teacher called each child's first name, and each one dutifully answered, "Present."

With hardly a signal from the teacher, younger students moved into the seats of the older ones to share songbooks. They sang two out of the Gospel Revival tradition—"Just As I Am" and "Shall We Gather At the River?" The German songs that they sing on Fridays come from their church repertoire. With speed and little expression, Mary read the Bible story about Jacob's sons going to Egypt to buy grain from the brother that they had sold into slavery and then asked, "What can you do when you want to erase something you did?" A fifth grader put up her hand and answered, "Ask God for forgiveness." The morning exercise,

ending with reciting The Lord's Prayer in German, concluded the religious teaching for the day. Among the blackboard assignments was memorizing a Bible verse by Friday—a typical practice in Amish schools.

School is to teach reading, writing, spelling and arithmetic with few frills.

TEACHING OF THE BASIC 3Rs

Mary tackled the day's schedule with directness. Arithmetic is the first subject of the day. Within one hour, she had taught each class a new mathematical skill—the fifth grade, dividing with three-digit divisors; the sixth grade, muliplying two three-digit numbers; averaging for seventh grade and the measurement of angles for those in their last year of schooling. Teacher Kline explained examples on the board, questioning each student for any lack of understanding—all with a sense of urgency.

She used routines to keep the pupils focused on their lessons. For example, after she called the fifth graders to bring their arithmetic books, she waited until they walked to a recitation bench against the side wall in a line just as they were seated. Moving promptly and in this order is one of the eleven rules printed in her schedule book. Now during the sixth week of school, it is a solid classroom habit.

Mary's life experience of 17 years is her training. As a girl, she played school a lot during the four years that her older sister taught. Mary's own interest and success as a scholar helped to make her a candidate when the former teacher at this school married. "I'm surprised how much (from my own eight years) comes back, especially the arithmetic."

And the basic skills that are taught remain the same year after year. The children use a 1934 math series that had been used by their grandparents in the 1920s. An Amish company in Lancaster County had gained persmission to reprint it for their parochial schools.

The fifth graders found quotients, using three-digit divisors. She questioned each student, including her own brother, as she went over the thinking process for this kind of division. When one boy's attention seemed to wander, teacher Kline reminded, "Follow along, Eli." She assigned problems; dismissed the six fifth graders from the reciting bench, and turned to visit each seat with a hand raised.

The seventh graders wrestled with averages, working out of books solid with exercises. It is no matter that the reading problems are outdated. Knowing the process to find the cost per mile of driving a car a certain distance when gas is 16.8¢ per gallon *is* important; that the figures are not realistic and that the students will not use horsepower that consumes gas pale behind the value of being able to find averages.

Eighth graders dug into their lesson on percentages, moving through 9 pages of arithmetic each week during their last year of formal schooling. Soon they will be measuring angles, areas and computing profit and loss—all essential for the woodcraft businesses that many Amish develop.

At recess, boys in dark pants and matching elastic straps pounded down the steps to the open area below. A few raced to the outhouses before they started playing Prisoners Base. Younger children from the other room dashed to see-saws that were long enough to flip a stomach. Older girls stayed working at their books. Rachel, a tall Old Order girl in a sea-green dress with an apron of the same knit but without a cape, went up front to copy an assignment that she couldn't read from her seat on this gray day. Amish usually refrain from lighting their gas or kerosene lanterns during day time.

Their reading books from an Amish publisher in Canada introduced the poems of Alfred Tennyson and Walt Whitman and included excerpts from The Proverbs, *Martyrs Mirror* and Rudyard Kipling's *The Jungle Book*. Comprehension of the material surpassed any need to interpret the writer's purpose or the piece's historic or literary significance. Amish parents want their children to leave formal school at age fourteen here in Ohio with the ability to read to get new information for earning an income.

One evening an Old Order man who has trained himself to research history and genealogies confided, "I just wish I could write better; I didn't have the interest when I was in school."

Naomi, a pink-cheeked rotund fourth grader, feels such boredom now. "I'd much rather be at home because there are so many interesting things to do." Who wouldn't agree that farm activities crackle with more adventure than learning by rote? The Amish condense school to the essentials so that their children can continue the path to self-sufficiency within their own faith community.

Amish children add their own spark to school. To get there faster, boys in Lancaster may ride ponies bareback or navigate on roller skates, wagons or scooters. Children who like drawing make pictures on their own.

USING INFORMATION SOURCES

To farm or run another business today, the Amish rely on professionals and other information sources.

Many Amish women selling quilts or baked goods from their homes ask me for sales contacts or suggestions for getting the word around. For technical information, they inquire from an engineer neighbor or the agricultural extension office or visit the public library. They target what they need to know and find it. They do not spout knowledge to put themselves in a good light. The Amish way is "to walk humbly with your God," learning essentials enroute. One valuable tool is the calculator, acceptable because it uses battery-stored electricity.

Doing Business At Peace With the *Ordnung*

East of London, Ontario inside the door of a new building marked by a straightforward sign, Pathway Publishers, a row of black bonnets and coats hung on hooks in a plain anteroom similar to my grade school cloakroom. In the next room about six Amish women from the community still clad in black hats and coats stood at several library book racks hunched over books or religious periodicals reading silently in very dim light. A press clattered to the side in a larger room where women in solid-colored dresses collated folded press sheets, stacked and counted the periodicals that instruct Amish teachers and guide and inform families. No radio music to spurs the work on.

A university graduate who became Amish is at the helm of this publishing enterprise. He contributed his journalistic skills and the ability to convert the power source of a Heidelberg press to air hydraulics. Headlines of the lead articles for the new issues printed in black and white without pictures instruct in points of Amish faith. The press provides a forum for exchanging viewpoints among the 130,000 Amish in North America.

SELLING SIX DAYS ONLY

For many a year, I've stopped by Amish farms advertising one or two vegetables or fruits, a household's surplus of potatoes or onions. A second unevenly printed sign usually announced, "No Sunday Sales." The Amish keep the "Lord's Day" as a day of rest not retailing. They do not buy or sell, not even a soda from a vending machine. They eat food that was prepared beforehand. They do not work at their job. (A minister is ordained by God, not hired by the district. He works or farms to bring in an income for his family.) Lacking education beyond eighth grade, the Amish do not deal with the round-the-clock shifts of the service professions.

EARNING APART FROM FARM LIFE

As farm prices soared and land for sale decreased in the eighties, the Amish adapted by establishing home businesses and cottage industries. A drive through Holmes County in Ohio or eastern Lancaster in Pennsylvania shows a variety of products. Signs offer such services as custom wood turning; plumbing with air water pumps and products such as hickory rockers; clothes drying racks; doll cradles and natural foods. Some of these enterprises grew in need of more production space and constructed a larger shop, still within walking distance of the house.

In a township in Lancaster where 95 % of the farmers are Amish there are over a hundred shops fielding their wares and services to tourists and other Amish. Farming and home industries both comply to a strong value of the Amish. The main purpose of a home is training children in the Amish lifestyle and principles. This can develop best on a farm because children can work alongside their parents with no outside influences, each one modeling his/her same-sex parent.

HOME BUSINESSES FOR PARENTING GOALS

Parenting, however, is a shared effort among the Amish. When Sadie Mae's three preschool girls lose interest in the contents of their toy chest or in imitating their mother, they skip across the backyard to their father's woodshop where he and a crew of relatives make porch swings, gazebos and picnic tables for wholesale orders. Rather than being sent away by their mother, they leave for diversion, being comfortable with either parent.

Three-year-old Jonas spends much of the day in the shop where his father saws, screws, and paints wood to build solid toys—wagons, ironing boards, doll beds and trucks. Brown-bearded Elam can see any customers through a window after a bell signals their arrival. He carries Jonas into the showroom, holding him in his lap at a small table as customers browse. Out comes paper and pencil to occupy the lad. Elam talks more to his small son than to the exclaiming tourists. The prices are incredulously low so the out-of-staters buy for their grandchildren. This craftsman's overhead does not include electricity, social security, media advertising nor a salary that must send his six children to music lessons, to car dealers and then on to university. Because his buyers come to his turf and on his terms, Elam and other craftsmen stay within their own world with his wife within earshot and a hot dinner at home when he puts up his Closed sign over the noon hour.

One cabinetmaker in Ohio has had so many orders for oak shelves, cupboards and tables over the last three years that he's had no need for a phone or sign at the shop. A member of the New Order group, which allows phones at home, he explains,"I don't want calls to interrupt production. I tell people to call me at the house early in the morning." Keeping things simple and focused is the Amish way.

WORKING AWAY FROM HOME

Unmarried young adults may "work away," meaning outside the home. Traditionally, girls did housework for relatives with new babies or cleaned for the English. Some with aptness for learning taught school until they married. More recently, Amish girls in prayer coverings, bright cape dresses and black footwear waitress at tourist restaurants; stand at market for a Mennonite stallholder or work as chambermaids at motels. Some families forbid this much contact with the outside world and fear that fancy objects or deceitful ways of co-workers may sway them from the church discipline. One parent said she only allows her children to work at places where there is a large group of Amish employees. And then only until they marry.

Young men often work with other Amish for an English builder or a roofer. The boss or a hired van provides transport to the work location. Even though a young man who is not yet a member may own a car during this period of "sowing his wild oats," he will not drive it to work. Adherence to the symbols dictated by the *Ordnung* counts much for one's good intentions. If one follows the expected Amish styles, colors of clothing and attends church regularly, for example, an action that varies from ordinary practice is more likely to be overlooked.

One self-trained artist whose original watercolors sell as quickly as she paints them does not promote her work. While she nourishes her skill by studying technique from library books and spending long days at exhibits, she would never do so on Sundays and always wears the Old Order garb.

She paints faceless subjects when she does include people in her scenics because she feels an inner conviction against "making graven images," the commandment that makes Amish frown on photographs and portraits. One woman confided, "But how we like to look for ourselves in pictures!"

HONORING THE *ORDNUNG*

One single lady strongly committed to her faith community but deeply desirous of training in a medical field proceeded to study practical nursing by correspondence while caring for ailing family members. She rejected nursing school because she would have had to live in the dorm and wear a regulation uniform. She wanted to remain Amish. In medical technology she would work in a lab out of the public eye and could wear her Amish garb. This was important to her and to the ordained leaders in her district.

She began hospital employment with an exemption from working on Sunday. Since nobody likes to work on weekends, she felt uncomfortable with her privilege. She decided to work without pay on off-church Sundays. By shaping her career inside the parameters of her community, this woman is at peace with the *Ordnung* and her God.

Amish who enlarge their businesses sometimes form a partnership or corporation with a non-Amish person. In one Ohio corporation that involved vehicles, the Amish shareholder sought permission for the alliance from his church district. His leasing rather than owning the company's fleet of trucks satisfied the leaders. This kind of business arrangement enables Amish to offer fax and 24-hour phone service as well as have outsiders handle advertising and promotion. A very savy group of Amish business people are successful with their enterprise and at following Amish ways.

Nurturing Family Ties and Community Connections

Sadie Mae apologized for her messy kitchen. I told her I was still smelling her roses along the walk and was pleased that she was home. My friend has no phone in her vicinity and so we communicate Amish style, by letter and personal visit. Both are more satisfying than talking to each other's answering machine.

I did notice that things were out of place. Windowside African violets and ferns crowded the table. Now cold for the summer, the coal stove propped window screens. The clock shelf was empty. And four women in solid purple, blue and green dresses were busy enough to be a work crew.

Such a typical Amish happening, but so foreign to mainstream urban culture! Four nieces had arrived to help their seventy-year-old maiden aunt, explaining, "We just want to do whatever needs to be done." Sadie Mae gave them some suggestions, and soon they were washing windows and woodwork and painting sash. They shared family news except pregnancies. The time to talk about a new little one in the Amish community is after the baby arrives, not while it's on its way.

Dinner, the 11 o'clock midday meal, was next door at Sadie Mae's sister-in-law's home. This *grossdaudi haus* served as a parking place for the preschoolers who came along but needed some distance from wet paint. The talk was comfortable. Sadie Mae described a lovely hour-long ride to a potluck at the farm of a neighbor who had moved to another part of the county. "The horse was so frisky, and we gabbed all the way up. There were so many different kinds of food." Childlike delight came through her voice.

Soon after two, the nieces put on their black bonnets and tucked their children into their carriages to get home before their schoolchildren. Without hurry or distress, they each untied and hitched a horse to a buggy. One infant howled while her mother bundled her into the arms of a passenger. One niece took to the lane on foot with her toddler in tow on a wagon. All departed in a peaceful flow, appreciative of a day together but hardly aware how extraordinary to be enfolded into such a family support system.

SINGLES WITHIN THE COMMUNITY

Families are so central to Amish community life

that single women are gathered more closely into the extended and church family. Rather than being abandoned to devise their own social experiences, they are invited to join others. When Naomi and John filled up a van to visit Longwood Gardens, they included John's sister Rachel.

When two sisters in their forties bought a home together, their parents gave them a large set of china as a house-warming gift.

Giving and sharing are natural results of caring, and the Amish who are both yielded and loving make these practices part of every day. Elam's two youngsters wheeled milk on their wooden wagon to their neighbor. The boys brought home some whoopie pies that did not sell at market that day.

The doctor recommended that Ella Mae do complete bedrest the last few weeks of her pregnancy. As soon as she informed her sister, Priscilla offered her seventeen-year-old daughter to help with the children and meals. She explained Mary's availability, "The stand is slow now, and she has some free time before she helps with Steve and Sara's wedding."

John's maiden sister, who lives in the smallest third of the *grossdaudi haus,* brings a small pitcher to the milkhouse each afternoon to fill it for her cereal the next morning. It is more valuable for John to share than for his sister to be independent.

When Susie drove by horse and buggy over to her daughter's to make applesauce, the apples were too green so they patched and mended clothes and turned tomatoes into sauce.

Ada sent company leftovers—a pie, pudding, pork barbecue and cabbage slaw— to her daughter's family living at the family farm down the lane. Ada explained her gesture, "Helping with the milking is enough for her just now." A mother of four, her daughter is eight months' pregnant.

The Church also extends helpfulness. When Joshua Yoder left a widow with five young children, she sold her horse to have a milking cow and accepted transportation from others.

Young people in a farming community butchered a beef and left the packaged meat on the porch of a church family that had suffered from a fire.

ON HAND DURING PERSONAL DIFFICULTIES

Marian had been paying into the Church's Hospital Aid Fund regularly for years. It is Amish practice to use this resource and one's savings when hospitalization is needed. The Amish do not have health insurance. Marian drew from this Fund when she needed a gall bladder operation. The deacons offered her the balance from the Alms Fund, but she preferred to make regular payments to the hospital when she went back to work. The Amish strongly oppose government handouts and insurances, insisting, "We take care of our own."

Leaders have pressed for their members to be exempt from paying into the Social Security Fund because they will not collect it. Since 1965 self-employed Amish qualify for exemption, and many with businesses structure the accounting so that each employee is self-employed. Those who work for non-Amish observe the deduction on their paycheck and wrestle individually with the issue of collecting.

Sixty-year-olds hesitate to discuss their own personal plans re: Social Security benefits with their family or friends. They hear the ministry call Social Security withdrawals, "unearned money." Amish leaders fear that "getting something for nothing" will erode the next generation's willingness to work and will diffuse their support for aging members. An Ohio employee regrets all the money deducted that he earned over 26 years of employment but will never use. "I'll let it there," he said, submitting to the way of his people.

One single woman from Lancaster said she will accept the money she has paid in because it's really hers, but she would prefer an automatic deposit into her account rather than having a check coming to her mailbox each month. Splitting hairs is bound to happen when a society prescribes behavior for individuals to conform to the group.

With or without Social Security payments, aging among the Amish lacks the distresses that plague many mainstream Americans. Regardless of care needs, an old person fills a place in the family until death. There are no Amish retirement homes. Parents plan to live in a *grossdaddi haus*, an extension of the main house built especially for grandparents. Three interconnected household units have been common so that the farm work can be shared. Sometimes parents build a small house on another part of the farm. Zoning laws in booming Lancaster affect some Amish building decisions. Amish parents would not retire with all their children living in distant settlements.

A PLACE FOR THE AGED

When parents are too feeble to manage their own household, they live with one of the children. My sixty-year-old friend in Wayne County has complete assurance that she will live with one of her children by and by—even if she needs total bed care. One ninety-year-old in Lancaster County enjoys rotating among her six children, a week at a time. "I get to watch them all grow without being there long enough to be a burden to any," she smiled. And how the preschoolers enjoy her stories and her patience with helping them "do things like grownups."

Acting out of traditional and Biblical assumptions, families flexibly bend to accommodate the needs of the aged. Rachel and Mary Lapp both lived with their parents in a town near Lancaster City but worked away from home. When their father suffered a stroke, they arranged their schedules so that one of them was always home. After his death, their mother's mind weakened so Rachel stayed home and baked for an income. The aroma of 720 dinner rolls warmed the house through the night to be fresh for restaurants. Her mother soon needed watchful care during the day when Rachel had slept after her marathon baking. She dropped the baking and earned by manually typing for an Amish publication. For Rachel and Mary, caring for their parents over almost 20 years was a privilege as well as an opportunity. Rather than putting their own lives on hold, they learned new skills at home in order to continue earning.

Now that *they* are approaching retirement, Rachel and Mary have moved near a younger brother who never joined the Amish church. (The ban does apply unless a family member had once been an Amish church member and left the Amish.) Besides enjoying family gatherings, they are conscious of being close geographically to someone who cares.

Family experiences build an attitude of parents and offspring wanting to be close throughout life. Farm life assumed that all children would spend their preschool years with either or both parents and frequent interactions with relatives. Church services, Sunday visiting and cooperative work projects supported the values of the parents.

When a boy got his horse and buggy at sixteen, and girls the right to date and "run around" with the young people, there were strong Amish ties directing them to socialize with their own rather than "being unequally yoked with unbelievers."

Church membership, work on the farm and a

home wedding with family and church friends strengthened commitment to an Amish lifestyle.

HOME WEDDING

In the Lancaster County settlement, an engaged couple chooses a Tuesday or Thursday in November for their wedding. More weddings, around 90 each year, over the past years of population growth force some to use an October or December date. Wearing a black covering and a plain dress styled like her Sunday garb, the bride comes downstairs with her black-suited groom and the ministers. She wears a new white cape and apron, two standard accessories for all that directly benefit the women who are pregnant or breastfeeding.

Without bulletins, flowers, candles, rehearsals, the service evolves in that private session. After the main sermon, the couple takes their vows, and a benediction closes the service. All the guests enjoy a superb meal, usually featuring roasted boneless chicken mixed into a savory filling.

The wedding itself allows no opportunity to showcase prosperity. It is one of the many community rituals that mark passage into new responsibilities. Before communion the next spring the husband will be growing a full beard, and the couple will be keeping house in their own place.They have closeted any

youthful attempts to experience worldly activities such as drinking; going to a professional ball game on Sunday; and replacing their Amish clothing with T-shirts or skirts and blouses. All those years of repeated community experiences reinforced Amishness. Contacts with outsiders were limited to occasional shopping trips; visits to the bank and brief encounters of selling eggs or surplus produce to passersby.

For young Amish born in the nineties, the winds of change blow across the traditions that are theirs from birth. Their European ancestors suffered persecution for their faith. No Amish remain there, but even here in America they have endured jail and harassment until they made peace with the government regarding their own parochial schools and exemption from high school and Social Security. Now the young ones grow up with innumerable opportunities to make money from tourists and other consumers who crave their well-made products. Whether they can continue farming in the burgeoning East or even will in the light of more remunerative jobs is a puzzler for the upcoming generation. Despite the changes in the workplace, their commitment to family and community--everyone taking care of each other--still holds firm. And that is Amishness in action.

Among the more than 100,000 Amish in North America, plain and modest dress, horse-drawn transportation and simple technology set these people apart from mainstream society. (FAR LEFT) Strong ties develop within each age group, especially after their sixteenth birthday when young people meet at social gatherings. Already "running around," as this socializing is called, these girls walk to a Sunday evening singing in Pennsylvania's Lancaster County. (LEFT) In eastern Ohio, the largest Amish settlement in the world, members of conservative and liberal groups interact at the weekly markets held at various villages. A New Order Amishwoman chats with a more conservative buyer at the Farmerstown Market. (BELOW) The Amish who migrated from Europe to southern Ontario in the early 1800s drive a topless buggy, a practice to indicate their boundary of "being separate from the world." Children who usually walk several miles to school in Milbank vicinity appreciate a ride home.

(FAR LEFT) Ohio farmers bring produce and baked goods in a utility wagon to the Wednesday market at Mt. Hope. Preschoolers spend their days with one or the other parent. (LOWER LEFT) From their early years, Amish children help with chores, slowly assuming responsibility for whole tasks. Painting fence at their family dairy farm near New Holland is a summer activity for these two siblings. (LEFT) Youth play volleyball at this young people's Sunday evening frolic. Open or courting buggies provide spectator seats and a stabilizer for the net ropes. (BELOW) Up to the grave, Amish people take care of their own. After a home funeral, relatives and friends wend their way to an Amish cemetery where a final service and viewing under the sky precedes the burial.

The Amish pace their lives to benefit from God's resources—and to enjoy His gifts. (LEFT) A soaring pulley line exposes Amish wash to a drying breeze. Sewn by mother to be buttoned rather than zippered, broadfall pants flap in the wind. The family seamstress often makes several garments from one piece of fabric. (LOWER LEFT) Lancaster tobacco dries in its airy shed while youngsters imitate the mode of transportation in their daily lives. It's even more fun to be a shoeless horse prancing through puddles! (LOWER RIGHT) Except for those keeping business schedules and appointments, Amish usually take time to visit. This pleasure strengthens their community—and, in this instance, gives Amish children in Ohio time to explore.

(PREVIOUS PAGES) Two women in a carriage with steel wagon wheels and a more conservative Swartzentruber Amish family in an open wagon slowly penetrate the morning fog that frequently settles into Holmes County's creek-fed bottomlands. (UPPER LEFT) From the earth Amish children help their English neighbors scoop up the potatoes. (BELOW) This Lancaster Amish woman works hard at her lawn and flower plantings. (UPPER RIGHT) The Amish ingeniously adapt the power sources permitted by the *Ordnung*, a largely unwritten but well-understood body of rules. Animal power is used to pull push lawnmowers, one to three at a time. (LOWER RIGHT) For generations the Amish have reaped abundantly from the earth by nurturing the soil and respecting God's timing. This young Amish couple stakes out their spring garden in Lancaster County.

(UPPER LEFT) Three generations in the garb of Ohio Amish wait for traffic in the town of Mt. Hope in Holmes County. The infant is wrapped in a *mandlie* or hooded shawl for warmth. (LOWER LEFT) When Amish cannot walk, they drive a horse and carriage, an activity that requires no license. Their horses' "exhaust" is also evident on a wintry morning. (UPPER RIGHT) The Amish like to spend time outdoors. This family walks in their Sunday clothes. The boy wears a black straw hat sold by Spector's, a Midwest store that caters to Amish tastes. (BELOW) Playing ice hockey follows the chilly task of scraping the snow off the farm pond.

(RIGHT) In southern Lancaster, a schoolboy intently walks toward a day at a wooden desk in one room with eight grades. (BELOW) Church leaders require that animals pull field implements although stationary engine-powered equipment is allowed. If tractors were permitted for field work, people may use them to run to town and gradually the car would be accepted—and Amish values threatened. At the edge of Lancaster's industrial development, a team of Belgian workhorses pull a haybine that has its own diesel engine to cut and bind alfalfa into bales. (FAR RIGHT) Amish farmers are self-educated about cropping, dairying and soil conservation. They turn to professionals when they need them. This veterinarian treats a cow suffering from mastitis.

(FAR LEFT) The stationary tractor that Amish in Lancaster use for belt power to thresh wheat and to fill the silo has steel-rimmed rather than inflatable tires. This standard forbids the use of bicycles and keeps modern living at bay. (LEFT) Roller skates and scooters are acceptable means of increasing foot power in Amish communities. Lancaster, PA. (BELOW) Working in the produce patch deserves a taste of the fruit of the vine, today a ripe watermelon for these young Amish folk in Lancaster.

(PREVIOUS PAGES) Amish driver, horse and buggy all move up an Ohio grade at a rate of 5mph. The Amish maximize the use of the sun from dawn to dusk. (BELOW) At sundown they allow themselves and their horse to think about quitting in Lancaster County; (LOWER LEFT) near Charm, a Holmes County town with a high percentage Amish population, and (RIGHT and FAR RIGHT) on Ontario's flatlands. (LOWER RIGHT) Dawn in Ohio graces a farmstead and its windmill for water power.

(PREVIOUS PAGES) Flaming skies above well-watered, tree-covered flatlands—all at an acceptable price from a welcoming government—drew the first Amish settlers from Europe to Ontario in 1824. (UPPER LEFT) Tobacco for cigars is a good but labor-intensive cash crop for some Amish farmers in Lancaster. Two female family members put the long, heavy leaves onto 48-inch lathes (BELOW LEFT) to hang in a tobacco shed for drying. (BELOW) A Canadian farmer harvests corn to cut into silage and to blow into storage for cattle feeding.

(BELOW) Amish farmers' skills include a knowledge of draft-powered machinery. This Lancaster farmer disks in spring while (LOWER LEFT) a lad drives a six-mule team pulling a disk harrow across a contoured field. (UPPER RIGHT) A sizable team is also necessary to pull the machine that rakes and binds alfalfa hay. (FAR RIGHT) During the first week of July shocks of Lancaster County wheat await a threshing ring of neighbors to finish the harvest. (LOWER RIGHT) A young Amish woman rakes hay with an implement manufactured especially for draft power.

(FAR LEFT) Fog cloaks a milk hack, a utility wagon designed by Ohio farmers to haul their milk cans to cheese factories. (LEFT) Snow can upset farm routines. This farmer rode bareback to the end of his lane to help a snowbound vehicle. (LOWER LEFT) Horses gladly return to the barn after an extended day of raking in the fields. The outdated equipment was repaired and customized for Amish use. (BELOW) An Amish farmer east of Milbank, Ontario, pitchforks straw onto a wagon pulled by workhorses. (LOWER RIGHT) Regardless of the complexities of living in a modern world, there is promise in Ontario skies.

(PREVIOUS PAGES) A Pennsylvania farmer exercises his draft horses on a prime day for sleighing. (BELOW) When spring sprouts a meadow of green grass and dandelions below a blossoming fruit tree, the Amish countryside invites everybody outdoors. (RIGHT) Spreading fertilizer and manure are springtime practices that informed Amish farmers do with careful calculations.

(RIGHT) Farm responsibilities for children increase as they become older. These children are helping to collect hay bales from the field. (LOWER LEFT) Transplanting and planting require careful soil preparation. (FAR RIGHT) German hymnals and prayer books used by Amish today hark back to their Anabaptist roots. With Mennonites and Swiss Brethren, they rebaptized adults who expressed faith.

HISTORY AND KINFOLK

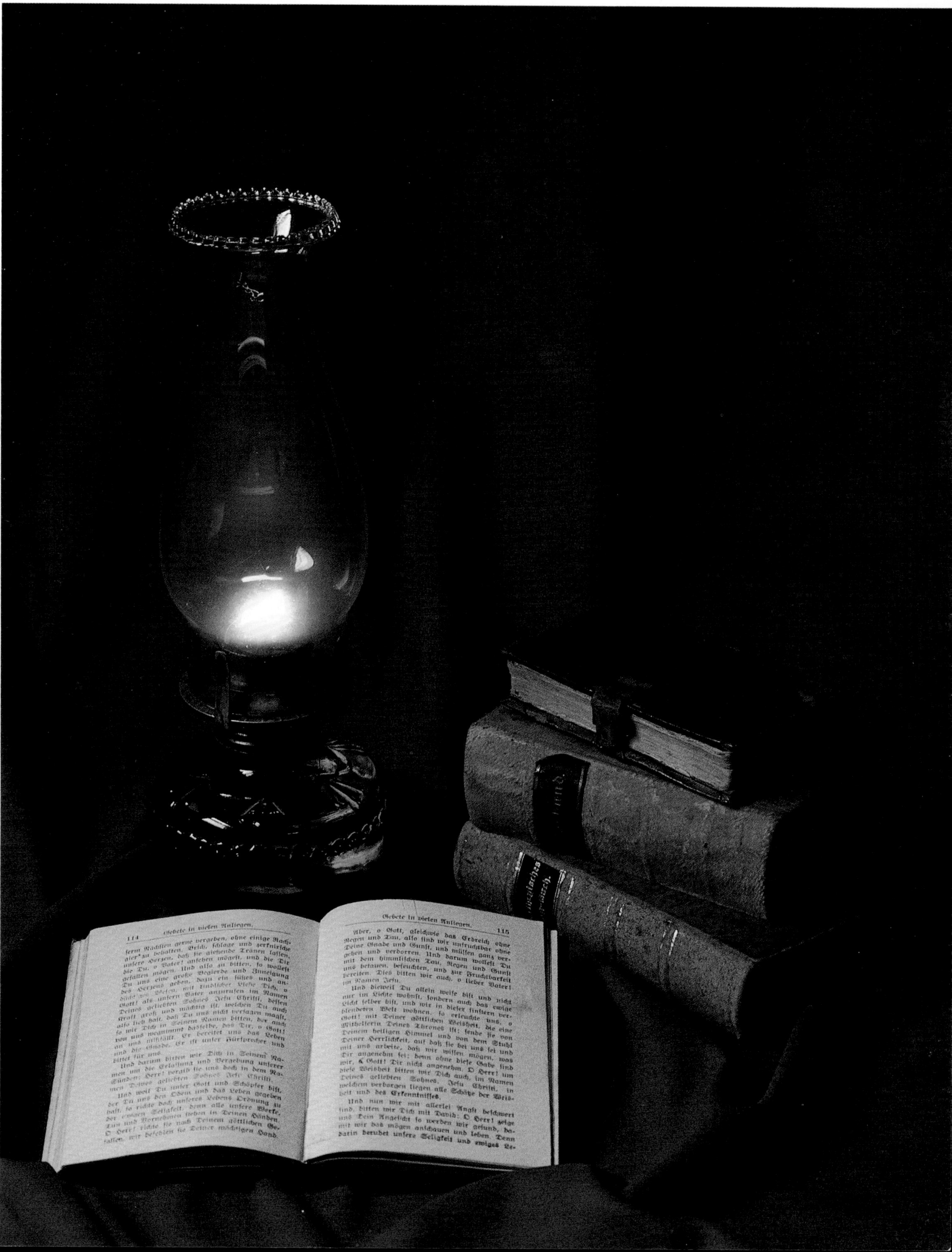

(LOWER LEFT) In their homes, Amish keep a *Martyrs' Mirror*, a thick record of persecutions suffered by European Anabaptists during the Reformation era. (RIGHT) The home of Hans Herr, a Mennonite bishop who settled in Lancaster around 1719, portrays the background of the Anabaptist immigration to Pennsylvania. Some were called Mennonites after a Swiss Anabaptist leader named Menno Simons. The Amish became their own Anabaptist group, taking a hardline position on dress and shunning those who left the Church. (FAR RIGHT) The Amish aimed for a simple, close-to-the-earth lifestyle set towards peaceful living. (LOWER RIGHT) As the Amish sought for a place where they could live their beliefs undisturbed, they accepted the land offer of William Penn. Other plain groups settled in Pennsylvania: Dundards, Quakers and Hutterites as well as the German Baptists who lived communally at Ephrata Cloister.

The Old Order Mennonite Church is a plain sect whose Biblical practices are similar to the Amish. At a barn-raising, volunteers covered the barn with a hip roof in one day. They dress plain; drive black buggies and maintain close family ties and church connections. (FOLLOWING PAGES) The barn-raisers ate a hearty dinner at noon in the Mennonite family kitchen.

(LEFT) The Amish find creative and practical ways to use vehicles and containers. A Mt. Hope lad gets a ride home with some groceries in a wagon made in Berlin, Ohio. (FAR LEFT) After putting something in the "carriage trunk," an Ohio preschooler "closes the curtain," so they say, with a snap. (BELOW LEFT) A handtruck hauls more than feed bags for two Lancaster teenagers having fun. (BELOW) Calves like much bigger bottles than babies, and two brothers are glad to wait for them to be filled for feeding two newborns in the barn.

lea lePP ist geborren den 12 den may
im iahr unzerres herren 1836 iohannes
kimmis ist geborren den 15 den märz
im iahr unzerres herren 1831 be ha-
ben uns in den estand den 8 den
märz im iahr 1854
× Franica Lapp 1863

FAITH AND TRADITION

FAMILY LIFE

PATHWAY BOOK CATALOG 1991

CONTENTS

Young Companion
October. 1990

BLACKBOARD BULLETIN
September. 1990

There are two ways
of doing wrong. One
is not to do
what we are
told. The

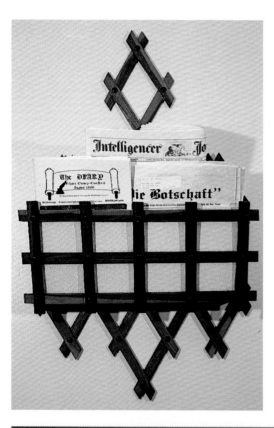

(FAR LEFT) The stories about the contents of a corner cupboard in an Amish home usually relate experiences that span several generations. (LOWER LEFT) Other handmade decorations bear a characteristic or two of the originator. The maker of this 1863 needlepoint sampler attached a lock of hair from her relatives near their initials. (LEFT) A Lancaster County *grossdaudi* (grandfather) constructed a hanging magazine rack from wood and carpet tacks for each of his grandchildren. This familiar fixture in an Amish home holds their favorite periodicals in both English and Pennsylvania Dutch, their dialect. (BELOW) The Amish homestead is a setting for creative and fulfilling work.

(PREVIOUS PAGES) Whether their drive near Milverton is for work or leisure, this Canadian Amish couple seems to find it delightful. (BELOW) Mailboxes often hold welcome exchanges with friends and relatives in other settlements. Recently some in Ohio wear both the husband's and wife's names; these in Lancaster note only the head of household. (RIGHT) A visit, expected or unannounced, means even more than a letter. (LOWER RIGHT) Even migratory martin birds are welcome at Amish homes in various states, here in Ohio. (FAR RIGHT) This church Amish girl decided to bring some of the blooms from their lovely chrysanthemum bed indoors. Some Amish also decorate with dried and silk flowers.

(UPPER and LOWER LEFT) Living at a slower pace without interruptions from phone, radio, TV as well as the noise of the dishwasher, vacuum and stereo gives Amish people the opportunity for aloneness and serenity. Exchanging farmlife for business puts many Amish into a work environment that may erode their lifestyle. (RIGHT) Even the communal effort of raising a barn symbolizes Amish apartness from mainstream values of individual success and competitive enterprise.

(LEFT, FAR LEFT and LOWER LEFT) Roads give Amish access to each other and the marketplace where they can meet members of other related groups as well as sell and buy. (BELOW) The Ohio system of having weekly market auction days creates a regular meeting place.

(PREVIOUS PAGES) In Milbank, Ontario, Amish buy seeds, protein-rich feed for dairy cows and grain when they need more than they raised. After parking her buggy in an open shed, this Amish woman walks to the grocery store across the street. (BELOW and RIGHT) The weekly markets in Ohio resemble a large Plain Folks convention. In addition to farmers selling their products, some wholesalers bring in shipped items such as pineapples and bananas. One rarely goes home without something.

(FAR LEFT) At the market in Kidron, Ohio, a Swartzentruber Amishwoman *(right)* is dressed more conservatively than the Old Order woman she's meeting. (LOWER LEFT) An Amish child hangs onto her mother burdened with purchases from Mt. Hope market. (LEFT) On any day the center of Mt. Hope is a crossroads for a steady flow of Holmes County Amish. (BELOW) Walking the long farm roads gives Amish time for thought and conversation.

(PREVIOUS PAGES) After a home funeral, Amish gather at the gravesite. (RIGHT) A funeral procession of Amish carriages enters Myers Cemetery in Lancaster County. (FAR RIGHT) Church friends dig two graves for members. (LOWER RIGHT) A funeral procession leaves the farmhouse after a funeral service and viewing where a light meal is served. Together family members have dressed the enbalmed body in white clothes. (BELOW) At a graveside service, the simple wooden coffin is opened for a viewing under the sky.

(LEFT) For church services, weddings and funerals, the Amish community convenes at the farmstead. (LOWER LEFT) As volunteers and supporters, Amish participate in local fire companies. Here an Amish family arrives at Witmer Fire Hall in Lancaster County for a fun-raising meal. (BELOW) Amish shield themselves from a summer downpour during a Lancaster farm sale.

(RIGHT) A couple travels home at sunset in the open carriage used by the Amish settlement west of Kitchener/Waterloo, Ontario. (LOWER RIGHT) Each settlement uses a distinctive style of carriage. Here the black closed buggies with roll-up side curtains belong to the Old Order Amish in eastern Ohio.

THE FAMILY PRODUCE

PUMPKINS -75¢ ea
Spanish Onions - 50¢ ea
Butternut squash 30¢ ea
Sheaves of corn

Thank you
for using bags ☺

(LEFT) An Ontario family offers surplus produce at a roadside stand at the end of their lane. (BELOW) Spring hoeing tidies a Lancaster County garden. (LOWER RIGHT) The large Amish kitchen table accommodates food preparation as well as meals and evening activities. (LOWER LEFT) The extended family, including grandmother, shares the work of snapping green beans on a summer evening in Lancaster County.

93

(PREVIOUS PAGES) Pears set in the back of a milk hack at an Ohio market. (RIGHT) Amish family gardens produce essential vegetables and an abundance of flowers. (FAR RIGHT) At Amish homesteads, here in Ohio, summer blooms brighten the gardens. (BELOW RIGHT) Home canned fruits and vegetables line cellar shelves for winter. (BELOW) In southern Lancaster County, Amish parents work together cultivating the family garden in the evening after farm chores.

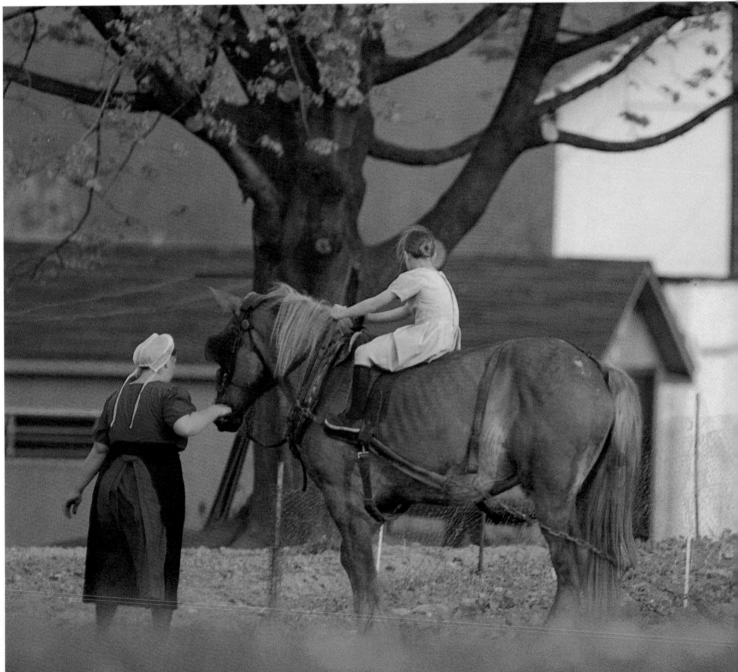

(FAR LEFT) This artful quilt displays many of the colors worn by the Amish. Quilts were originally pieced from fabric scraps. (LEFT) This "Love Birds" pattern features appliques and a quilting pattern that enhances it. (BELOW) This Amishwoman traces the quilting pattern onto a finished top.

(BELOW) A quilt hangs on a line in the countryside. (RIGHT) A modern quilt made in the "Tulip Basket" pattern is sold by an Amish businesswoman in her Bird-in-Hand shop in eastern Lancaster County. (FAR RIGHT) Amish women quilt together at a sewing circle that provides bedding and clothing to needy people. (FAR RIGHT) The simplicity of this quilt pattern, "Amish Bars" is in demand by non-Amish quilt buyers. While preparing their hope chest, Amish girls prefer more fancy patterns.

(PREVIOUS PAGES) Besides the mixed product line retailed at this shop in Intercourse, this coach shop restores and customizes antique and new carriages. (BELOW) This original watercolor was painted by a self-taught Amish woman of Lancaster County. (LEFT) The interior of a mini-shed displays the dried herbs and flowers. (BOTTOM) In this sewing room, a Lancaster County single woman makes pillows and wall hangings. (FAR LEFT) A shop near Milbank manufactures carriages.

(BELOW) These quilted and painted clocks hang among other Amish-crafted items that sell to the booming tourist market in Lancaster County. (BOTTOM) Many businesses in Amish settlements provide products and services particular to the Plain People. One Amish company in Lancaster manufactures these farm implements adapted for draft power. (RIGHT) In metropolitan markets Amish make and sell highly prized food stuffs, here pretzels in Harrisburg, Pa.

Amish parochial schools operate under the direction of parents and focus on learning the 3 Rs. (LEFT) A teacher welcomes her students into their one-room Amish schoolhouse in rural Lancaster County. (FAR LEFT) Ontario boys walking from school stop a moment in front of a field of cut grain. (BELOW) Amish girls energetically stride to school in eastern Ontario.

(RIGHT) The no-frills structure of this Amish schoolhouse in Milbank, Ontario, is compatible with a curriculum to teach the children how to read, write and do math problems. (BELOW) These children enjoy fine September weather before the Canadian winter sets in. (FAR RIGHT) Wrapped in her Amish shawl, this young Canadian girl reflects a humble self-awareness. (LOWER RIGHT) This young man of Ontario looks ahead to his formal education ending soon after he has become a teen. (FOLLOWING PAGES) Lancaster County Amish children wait to cross Route 340, a congested tourist route in the heart of Amish farmland .

(BELOW) Playing ball occupies many a recess at an Amish school in Lancaster County. (LOWER LEFT) An Amish classroom seems like a relic from yesteryear. While first graders in pinafores practice printing at the board, other grades do seatwork. The teacher works with a reading class. (FAR LEFT) Two Lancaster County lads travel to school on skates. (LEFT) A family member picks up these children at school.

(BELOW) Jumping during recess warms these Amish scholars at Musser School in Lancaster County. (RIGHT) The spectators at this ball game in an Amish schoolyard use the pale fence as bleachers. (BELOW) "When the ball hits the bat,..."Amish boys relish this recess activity. (FOLLOWING PAGES) Against a field of mustard, an Amish boy disks another to break into and turn over sod for the next planting.